DEAD DOGS
DON'T BARK

...and they don't bite

A COLLECTION OF POETIC WISDOM
FOR THE DISCERNING
(SERIES 2)

by:

TOLU' A. AKINYEMI

Proofreading and Editing by Gabrielina Gabriel
(The Roaring Writer Ng.)

Typesetting by Word2Kindle

Design by Lola Betiku
LABET.MAKES.ART

Published by T & B Global Concepts Limited
ISBN: 978-1-9998159-2-9

Email:
tolu@toluakinyemi.com
author@deadlionsdontroar.com
author@tolutoludo.com

Website:
www.toluakinyemi.com
www.deadlionsdontroar.com
www.tolutoludo.com

ALSO, BY TOLU' A. AKINYEMI

"Dead Lions Don't Roar"
(A collection of Poetic Wisdom for the Discerning)

"Unravel your Hidden Gems"
(A collection of Inspirational and Motivational Essays)

Dead Cats Don't Meow
(A collection of Poetic Wisdom for the Discerning Series 3)

COMING SOON
Tolutoludo's Fables (A Collection of Short Stories for Children)

DEDICATION

Dead Dogs Don't Bark is dedicated to the Arts Council England for believing in my talents and to my Champs, Isaac and Abigail – "the world is your oyster", go forth and conquer.

CONTENTS

PREFACE

Dead Dogs Don't Bark is my third published work, and second collection in my Poetic Wisdom for the Discerning Series after Dead Lions Don't Roar, and my collection of motivational essays, Unravel your Hidden Gems.

This book will leave an imprint on you irrespective of your age or status as these are unique words that have been specially written because of you. Everyone will find it enthralling and I see it as the start of a revival – you wouldn't be wrong to call it a catalyst to the new. My main aim with Dead Dogs Don't Bark and the Poetic Wisdom for the Discerning series is to nurture other budding talents to put their gifts and talents to use.

Publishing three well received books in one year might not be the norm in most parts of the world; however, the aim is to raise a new generation of people who are happy to write their own story and do not live their lives on the opinion of others. Whether you are reading my new collection in school, at the office, during the holiday, or at home, I am sure there will always be something to take away, something new to learn from my repertoire of inborn wisdom.

I have written these poems in hope that they will inspire you, yes YOU, that person reading this book – to put your gifts to use. It doesn't just have to be writing a book as each one has a peculiar gift. Let's look at it this way: if Tolu' Akinyemi can do this, then you also can. In truth you can even do better, in your own niche with your distinct giftings.

Dead Dogs Don't Bark will help you attain new heights. It will teach you to embrace excellence. It will inspire you to be the best in your field of endeavours. To the young person, it will help you face your fears in boldness and conquer new grounds effortlessly. My books are life-changing, and they will leave you better and impart your knowledge.

As you can see the trend in my two Poetry Collections "Dead Lions Don't Roar" and "Dead Dogs Don't Bark" the message remains the same: we all have our Unique Roar and permit me to add "Bark". We are not just meant to add to the statistics and the World Population, but also to be the Change, the difference within our community, family and workplace.

Quit making excuses about lack of time; remember that everyone has twenty-four hours in equal proportion. Being busy should not be an excuse for not getting started. Quit procrastinating as this has led to the death of many great ideas right before they were birthed. Dead Dogs Don't Bark will help us to find our Unique Bark figuratively in our everyday living, work, business, relationships, marriages, and put our talents to beneficial use.

Literally speaking, being alive means we can do something worthwhile with our lives. We should not just be happy to count the days without making the days count. Always remember that the only time you can leave your footprints on the sands of time is when you are alive as the title infers, Dead Dogs Don't Bark.

As you go on to read through the pages of this book, which I have written specifically for you, I do hope that you will find it fulfilling and a great read as much I have enjoyed writing it.

ACKNOWLEDGEMENTS

Writing Dead Dogs Don't Bark is immense for me as Dead Lions Don't Roar finally has a sequel and a worthy one at that. Life as an Author means I need people to read my books and support my gift and I have found that with a great bunch of outstanding people in my life. Without their support it would not have been a leisurely ride.

Thanks be to God Almighty for the grace to write another book and the ability to continue to impact my generation positively. Special thanks to my darling wife and partner, Olabisi: I appreciate the support, feedback and encouragement. You truly deserve all the good that comes your way. Please, know that I will always love you.

A big thank you to my darling Isaac and Abigail, thanks for your understanding whenever I require my Quiet time to churn out new verses from time to time. In life, always be bold to face your fears and conquer new grounds. You can surpass my legacy and do greater works. The world is your oyster; go forth and conquer. You have my unalloyed support always.

Special thanks to my wonderful parents. All the great virtues and ideas I churn out today through my books are a function of the great investments and tutoring at your feet. I reminisce in joy when I think about all those years and beautiful memories which I will forever treasure.

To Olusola – In love, unity and brotherhood; our bond none can break. To Oluseyi – You are a superstar, the world awaits the manifestation of your glory. Let it out, you have so much in you. To Iretioluwa – My shining star, you are the definition of excellence. I will always cherish you and your lovers – Segun and David, they deserve top marks. To my In-laws, the Osiyoye's family – It's been amazing being part of the family and doing phenomenal things.

A special word of thanks to Ayodeji Omogunsoye and Emmanuel Osikilo, Funmi Ogunleye, Tayo Adebiyi, Evelyn Aneni, Abi Oguntubi, Oluwalayo Adetona, Seye Morakinyo: thanks for the support and encouragement always. Thanks for believing in me and what I represent.

A big thank you to the beautiful Anthonia Brown. I love everything you represent, the love of God, beauty and Intelligence. My wish for you in life is the very best. A big thank you to Olugbenga Obakin, Oladapo Arofin, Daniel Dada, Olalekan Owoeye, Bartholomew Akinwale, Rabiu Wasiu, Abodunde Ojikutu, Hakeem Olagunju, Nzubechukwu Alutu, Mustapha Apooyin, Ayo "Huggies Zubair, Bandele Okunowo, Aaron Lee, and Kenneth Robson (aka Kenny Toludo). Thanks for coming through and supporting me always.

Special thanks to the team who did a phenomenal job to bring my book to life, Gabriel Gabrielina and her team at The Roaring Writer for detailed proofreading and editing; Nick Caya and his team at Word2kindle for a wonderful Job", Lola Betiku for designing amazing book covers and Deborah Jayeola the brain box behind the cover ideas.

Special shout out to all the Poets I have shared a stage with at one time or another, most especially in the North East of England. And for all the feedback I have received which was to make me better. Sincere appreciation to Kirsten Luckins, Ken Brady, David Roe, Sky Hawkins and Mandy Maxwell: thanks for supporting my talent and craft; you will never be forgotten.

Special thank you to everyone who has given me a stage to shine and a platform to showcase my talent and a word of thanks to Antonia Brindle: together we have achieved amazing results.

Final appreciation and shout out to Yaya Toure, a true African Legend: thanks for supporting me in a distinct way". You are very much appreciated, and words are not enough to say thank you.

POEMS

CHAPTER 1

THE VOICE IN MY HEAD

The voice in my head was so fierce
Like the legendary Muhammad Ali's punch in his heydays
Before it was tainted by the chorus of not good enough by a select few
Like rainwater discoloured by the rusty roofing sheet.

I look in the mirror and see a shadow of my once boisterous self
More meat, fish and proteins
I screamed
The invisible monster was not a creation of the malaise of hunger.

There are days I look up the dictionary
For the synonym of failure
Enslaved by the **INSECURITIES** of my adversaries
Is this a war?

Where are the instruments of war?
It is a "war", I thought aloud
A war against dreams
Flailing ego and dream killers.

I have learnt to shake off the voices in my head
that want to silence the melody in my song
blur my bass
and turn my tenor to soprano.

When you hear me barking in the street corner
always remember that I have won and lost battles
with the voices playing discordant tunes in my head.

BOSS-WOMAN

We brought to the bench
Much more than the menu card on your dinner table
We were the larger than life

Colossus that took the walk of glory
Not on esplanade
But behind the closed door of board rooms and corporate hallways.

Call me **woman**
The professional woman
That epitomises everything in the realm of excellence.

If I were a football team, you will be screaming galacticos
Before you call me pretty and beautiful
See me as a spring of ideas

An ocean of knowledge
And the calming force that abuts it all together.

FOR THE LOVE OF WHITLEY BAY

In the seafront I discern the sound of rushing water
Remember the tale of stationary Ghost Ships turning our shoreline to a parking lot
Tidal waves dancing in rhythmic steps breaking steely barriers
The cool breeze caressing the evening moon.

Whitley is the lovers' nest
Lenses kissing nature with steamy eyes screaming love-struck
Vivid imagery of immortality
feasting through gaping eyeballs.

The nemesis of the postman
Oppugnant of Whitby
The blue sea gently massaging my aching feet
treating me to a love feast like a love-sick whippersnapper in need of affection.

In the playhouse
Laughter bags
crackled through the concrete walls
Humans roaring to flowery cantos.

All for the love of Whitley Bay.

AFFORDABILITY THERMOMETER

My affordability thermometer is screaming from bills that are
a creation of the ills in our society
I am viewed from the lens of a cash cow
the type they call 'money miss road' in my fatherland.

My cow of cash is neither malnourished
nor in need of being milked by those who
thrive in creating bills and even more bills
to my burgeoning net spend.

These days I view credit applications with deep suspicion
How can a lender derive joy in keeping me
in a cabinet of debt, throwing the keys away?
Keeping my misery barometer on a high.

If you want to fan the embers of my fury
wave the carrot of credit in my eyes
and you will see beyond the iris an eye which is at a crossroad
for being kept in the lid of debts that were once a creation of my greed
for things I may never ever need.

I am at the doctors again
For another affordability test and the only prescription is
"Buy what you can afford"
Three times daily
This is the only remedy to keep me in the kingdom of happiness.

"Money miss road" is a phrase commonly used in **Nigeria** to refer to a person
who has **money** but doesn't know how to spend it.

BLURRED

On the cusp of glory.

Flowers with leaves flourishing
before my candle was snuffed out
While I was wide awake.

Dreams charred
My life's smoke went out in a flash
as soon as my water evaporated.

There are moments I wished
I had numinous powers to vanish
When caught in the web of a crash.

Fading memories like silent pillow talk.

Play, pause and rewind
Fast-forward and the void is a gaping hole.
Memories and pictures litter the conservatory.

Your voice echoes
Dead Calm
And even more silence.

My nose bleeds from the scent of you
And water lilies well up in my belly
At our forever which has now been left in tatters.

Your love was the labyrinth
Now I wish this blur
was all a dream.

INDIVIDUAL AFFAIR

Don't see the world through the eyes of prerogative
like there are unpaid credits
about to pitch tent in your bank account.

No one is beholden to help you masticate
when the quest for survival becomes a hard nut
and emancipate you from the throes of poverty.

There are days we want to throw a banquet of *pity*
with friends and foes feasting and salivating
at the sordid tales and fails that have been our life's story.

Life is a school of hard knocks
With heavy punches that might throw us on the canvas
With the bell of failure screaming **SURRENDER!**

Drown the voices of perdition that sounds like an orchestra
playing a Sunday school hymn
inside your cerebrum.

I view life from the lens of an *economist*
The opportunity cost and alternative foregone hold me by the jugular
in those days all I have to caress is my cataclysms.

This is the précis and the culmination
Before you start the feast of pity, blameworthiness and finger pointing
Always remember that ***life is an individual affair***.

METAMORPHOSIS

I spent my adolescence plotting escape routes
and getting reprimanded for all types of misdemeanour
There are days I seat on the car bonnet
staring into the evening sky.

I communed with the stars
in strange tongues
I was a rollercoaster of personas
Introvert. Ambivert. Extrovert.

Fast forward.
I am a man on a mission
At war with my flops
Whose shadows are ever lurking.

I hear a silent dash - **Be bold to face your fears
and courageous to conquer new grounds.**

WHY SORRY?

Why sorry?
When you are not from Surrey?
And you don't live in the storey.

Why worry?
When you are not from Warri?
O'boy wetin you dey yarn na story.

So boring
Yes, I know you are roaring
Yes, I know, but I'm not sorry.

Warri city is an oil hub in South-South Nigeria,
known for its slangish type of English called pidgin.

O'boy wetin you dey yarn na story is a Warri slang meaning
"Young man what you are saying is a story.

INDELIBLE MARKS

Life has taught me that you need to leave
Indelible marks so visible
like stretch marks on a pregnant woman's belly.

It's cushy to become a wanderer
Or a rudderless being
In our fleeting and transient life.

There are days I seek to wipe every trace of sorrow
And every colouration
Of the misadventures of my youth.

With every breath in my olfactory nerves
The rhythmic sound of my heartbeat
And the dawning of a fresh day.

I am in ecstasy at the chance to leave indelible marks
So visible like tribal marks on an Egba man's cheekbones
On the sands of time.

Egba: A Yoruba speaking people of Southwestern Nigeria
chiefly concentrated in Abeokuta.

NEWCASTLE – THE CITY OF MY SHINING STAR

I have sojourned into cities that swept off the imprints
From my shoe sole in an instant
As soon as it felt my flagging steps.

Amongst cities, Newcastle was the temple
If Newcastle was a damsel
I will be roaring out *ear-splitting*, "Will you say 'I do'?"

Allow me to romanticize a city that brought out my flairs
From the rubbles of ineptitude
And set me on a high pedestal, **roaring** like a lion.

I once found home within familiar territories that became extinct
As the quest for survival tossed me to and fro
And I became a lesser being to those who once saw me as Noble.

A community of writers sheltered me
in the days the nights were forlorn
Poetry was my anthem and the verses my soul dances to.

I hope you will find your *"Newcastle"*
Your place of rest from all the baggage of slogging
That made your once tender shoulders heavy.

Newcastle was the *"city of my shining star"*
The city where the **riddles, puzzles and mystery** of my life
finally formed like an embryo in an ovulating woman.

DIS-UNITED STATES OF "A"

We are supposed to be the United States of A
But we are far from being United
Gun violence
Of catastrophic proportions
A reminder of our disunity
Racial divides
Still evident
Intolerance of the other
Now a given
We are gradually losing
Our toga
Of the world's big brother
A home for all
Trade wars
All to settle scores
Border walls
The new swansong
The Trump
Is now a lump
In our throats
We are supposed to be the United States of A
But we are far from being United.

OPINIONS

I have been beguiled with semantics that sounded like gospel
The truth found home in divided opinions and came out looking poor
It was labelled falsehood.

These days I don't know what to believe
as my brain has been twisted from differing Ideologies
that were once termed wise counsel.

A lot of humans have been lost in the sea of sentiments
And opinionated personas
The alpha of knowledge and encyclopaedia of all wisdom.

These days I go around with a sieve
To screen every fibre of opinion
And I tread chivalrously with cognizance that opinions are cheap.

PARENTING

It's five-thirty a.m.
My phone alarm is vibrating in its customary manner
that has now become a humdrum.
I drift into a trance
One last chance before I make way to the broods
which will always be a beehive of activities.
I think about poo, bath water, arguments over shower
Request for hugs and rekindling of love.

Raising up a king and a queen is a treasure.
My eyes squint
I remember the pain that hung me in the throes
Hyperemesis gravidarum
These days it drives me crazy
the noise, the questions, the craving for attention
My peace, I'm in dire need of
Solitude.

My mind needs chastening
This den will be a necropolis
without the clatter of toddlers
It's seven a.m.
Driving off for another day
No two days will ever be the same.

CAMOUFLAGE

How dare you wear a camouflage?
In my fatherland
A cloth so revered
Adorned by a select few
A badge for the battle ready
Many a time they are weary.

How dare you wear a camouflage?
Without a military badge
A hot slap
To the face
You could be left rattled
Like a soldier who has just lost a battle.

How dare you wear a camouflage?
If you are not brave-hearted
As the camouflage is not adorned by the faint.

The outcome might be a rain
Of tears and pain
Disgrace and Shame.

STAY TRUE

Stay true to your conviction
To your beliefs
And your calling.

Stay true to your vision
Mission
And purpose.

Stay true to yourself
You are at your best being who you are
Not anyone's photocopy
Or imitation.

Stay true to you.

YOU ARE BEAUTIFUL

You are beautiful
just the way you are
You are fearfully
and wonderfully made.

Listen, darling!
Shut out those voices
That seek to destroy your self-esteem
Your self-worth.

As you are beautiful
Just the way you are.

DON'T BULLY

Be a bright shining light
Like a solar powered bulb on full beam
Be a shoulder so big
Others can lean on in times of trouble

Through your words
Be a sparkle
A gemstone
And a lover

Face your personal demons
Don't quiver
At the slightest challenge

When life serves you lemons
Make lemonades so sweet
Your taste buds are aroused

Don't be a bully
An unheralded dimwit
It's all folly

The little clusters of mischief
The adventures
Rooted in youthful exuberance

Laced with ignorance
Could hinder us
From featuring in our own big circus.

Don't bully others, be a shining light and a good example to your generation.
To those who suffer from abuse and bullying, don't succumb to the voices of
oppression.

BULLIONS IN BOURDILLON

Your anti-money laundering laws are inert
when politicians parade cash laden
bullion vans in broad daylight.

I do not adorn the garment of a political activist
Neither am I sanctimonious to put to the sword
The political class who are renowned for chomping the national cake
than the task of nation building.

Incase, the internet forgets about the bullions in Bourdillon
let me remind you through these pages
the absurdity of the ruling class
and an affront on the teeming masses who wallow in abject poverty.

An easy way to get away with murder
Loot the national treasury or do the unthinkable
like the tales of bullions in bourdillon
as long as you are a member of the ruling party
you become untouchable from the long hands of the law.

We saw bullions in bourdillon
But no one dares question the lion.

PHARISEES AND SADDUCEES

The Pharisees
Are definitely not from the Far East
The Sadducees and their brothers in arms
Are the sadists that inhabit
Our very lives
They are the ones that gravitate
Towards the unimaginable
With questions that border on idiocy
And unreasoned
They are the ones who prefer you dead
Attend your rites with sombre faces
Crying more than the bereaved
It's a shackled grief.

They are the holier than thou
The perfect one
Who can do no wrong
They are the ones with the loudest voice in the prayer room
Engaged in a shouting match as if they are in a war zone
They are the ones that follow tradition to the letter
No matter whose ox is gored
As it makes them feel better
They are the ones that question your every move
Like a monitoring spirit
They are the definition of hypocrisy in present, past and future tense.

SLEEPING DEITY

Who will wake up the sleeping deity?
Amadioha
The god of thunder
Is as silent as Atan Cemetery on a dark rainy night.

In hushed tones the people whisper
The revered and feared
Is a mere shadow

this is an aberration
A cacophony of
Tears and Wailings.

Discordant tunes
Pounding like yam with Mortar and Pestle
All for the sleeping deity.

Amadioha is amongst the most popular of Igbo deities of the Igbo people of South-eastern Nigeria.

Atan Cemetery is a civil cemetery in Lagos, Nigeria which contains the largest concentration of World War II era war graves in Nigeria.

BEATEN

I have been beaten
Beaten in the world
With words
I take solace in my words
Verses
And rhymes
To hide
My bruises
Scars
And marks.

MILESTONES

I raise a glass cheering on my milestones
Before I take a rest and I'm laid still in my tombstone
While here celebrate the little feats
Create your own beats.

My inner demons communed with me *"Be humble"*
I'm scared this success is about to crumble
There are nights I dance with my shadow
Blooming in the rain like a fresh tomato.

There are days I war with the **demons of not good enough**
We wrestle
There are nights I sing **enough is enough**
With a melody of I am a chosen vessel.

Today I choose to celebrate **my milestones**
Before I'm laid still in **my tombstone.**

AGE

The way the days of my life accelerate like Usain Bolt
in his prime leaves a bitter taste on how fickle the days of man are
I look into the mirror and I see my alter ego yelling **RUN YOUR RACE**
As the clock of my life does tick tock with every passing second
The fear of death leaves me in rage that with every breath I take
the pages in the book of my life are diminishing.
I remember with fond memories my childhood
The metamorphosis
And all I see is that I am one step closer to the grave
with every passing day.

Goodbye to the innocence of childhood
To the momentous mistakes of my youth
I sit aloof with folded hands in my rocking chair
Waiting for the day of farewell
The end of the chapter.

STRANGER

Your sons cry for a father-figure
A mirror-image
Your daughters come home to silent walls
And dusty pans.

Your sons are haunted by the ghost
Of peer pressure
Your daughters hunt for tender care
In strange spaces.

Your house reeks of cracks
And holes
Your sons look you in the eyes
And say hello stranger.

MANCHESTER

Man, of Chester
Timber
And calibre.

SIXTY

Sixty is the year to reminisce
On life and its essence
On love and laughter
The fun, tears and banter.

Sixty is the year to revel
In the glory of the years past
Look back and marvel
And savour all the beautiful memories.

Sixty is the year to see the bright side
Jump on flights
Take a tour of the world
And recreate a whole new bond.

Sixty is the year of the new vista
Unbreakable by travails
It's not a time to despair
Unleash your diamond, humming like its jubilee.

PROCRASTINATION 2

Procrastination was the death knell
Our love turned sour
This was downhill.

Procrastinating was the catalyst
The fall
Of the castle that came crashing down.

Procrastination ended it all
Candles burning brightly
With the world to conquer.

Procrastinating was her getaway
Her leeway
And her legacy.

Procrastination was the end of us
My only remembrance
Of her.

The first part of this Poem was Published in "Dead Lions Don't Roar".

YES, YOU CAN

Banish those voices that say you can't
The voices that say you are not good enough
Listen, son
Hear me out, young lady.

You are a star
Whom no one can mar
You are unique
Distinct
Outstanding
Embodiment of all brilliance.

Go forth and conquer.

UNFOLLOWER

Your followers count so robust like active red cells
in my bloodstream
Yet, your following stats is low
like a man besieged with low sperm count.

I treat those who follow to unfollow
with deep-rooted antipathy
That's treachery
An intent to fleece in a normal way.

My phone toots again
And it's a follow notification from the serial unfollower
My mind screams *ignore*
This account has no room for two-faced people.

A sarcastic poem to the serial unfollower on social media.

CANCER

No one wants to fight a combat from a trailing position
In time immemorial, cancer diagnosis
was like a judge handing out a death sentence to a convicted criminal.

In these days there is always a fighting chance
The stigma is fading like the retreating sunshine
making way for the evening moon.

The cancerous cells may make my body a habitat
But my heart is a paradise of happiness
And a home of love.

Cancer is not a dead end
Don't be beguiled by the fallacy of statistics
And be consumed by the sheer agony of defeat.

Cancer will someday be where it belongs
The dustbin of history
Never to be seen again.

A WOMAN'S ANATOMY

To win a woman's love and earn her respect
is not about flexing muscles
And reeking in the filth of age long tradition.

It's in the facile understanding of the anatomy of a woman
The language of her heart
The meaning of unsaid words and her silent tears.

It's in giving her room to vent pent up angst
The unexpressed feelings and mood swings
All form part of a woman's anatomy.

Whoever unlocks this virtue has found a gateway to paradise.

INCONCLUSIVE

Inconclusive is the child of circumstance
that has been bastardised by politicians unwilling to vacate
the money minting machine that public office bears semblance to.

There are times you wonder why the garment of Third World
is fitting for some countries
like a well knitted slim-fit suit.

It's because mediocrity has been engraved
across all spheres
inconclusive became our lot.

Let me re-echo an easy way to sit tight in office
from the manuscript of our political Lords
Unleash violence and thuggery on election day.

Cause upheaval and snatch ballot boxes
and the seed of those vices will be inconclusive.
We have been enslaved by the dogma of inconclusive.

History won't be kind to all those
who left nation building on the periphery.

I AM FIRST A NIGERIAN

I am first a Nigerian
In creed and deed
Through my bloodstreams

I am first a Nigerian
By birth
And Heritage

I am first a Nigerian
My survival stories
Tell it all

I am first a Nigerian
Now a global citizen
Lending my voice
Art and talent
To make the world a better place.

I pledge to Nigeria my country, to be faithful, loyal and honest,
to serve Nigeria with all my strength,
To defend her unity, and uphold her honour and glory.
So help me God.

TROUBLED BUT NOT ALONE

Troubled but not alone
When you feel lonely pick up the phone
Life is full of ups and downs
Shove your adversity aside like a stranger thrown out of town.

Troubled, it's not the end
It's only a matter of time you will see the bend
I promise to lend you a hand
Till your mental health issue outlives its span.

Troubled, don't despair
Everything will be alright like the stars laid bare
Life's issues come with an expiry date
The abyss is not your fate.

Troubled, keep hope alive
Dance in the rain, don't look behind
Your mental health issue is now in the past
Cheers to victory at last.

SELF-LOVE

There are days I fall in love with my voice
My shadow
and the divergent intersections
that has become a part of my life's journey.

PRESSURE

No space for lazy hunks
If all you want is slumber
I'll kick you out like a malfunctioning computer
Pressure is not always bad
You might think it is out of fad
Leave me to play my cards
The lazy ones see me as ruthless
The smart workers see me as tireless
The results speak for us, that's matchless
Some left with thanks
With a work culture that is top-rank
As long as you do your tasks
You can survive anywhere with no cracks
A solid work ethic and you will make an impact
Don't leave anything to chance
Give it your best, remove the masks
And you could be dancing away to the bank
Possibly take me on a trip to France.

HOLIDAY

My heart is overshadowed by silent tears
when I see people of little means embark on holidays.
Of what use is a holiday fostered on the altar of credit

With identical siblings with similar names
Overdraft. Loans. Credit Cards.
I remind myself of my pledge to stay off the temptation

Of a holiday that keeps me in the pit of debt.
I reminisce on why people with their own hands
Dig the pit of debt.

Throwing themselves under the rubbles.
It's payback time
The veil is off and they are consumed by a whirlwind of debts.

The tribute
Home might be a blessing, till my bills lessen.

EXCELLENCE

Cuddle up to excellence
Else mediocrity can catch up with you like a heatwave
Released in full force like a loaf oven baked
The days of long service awards are over
If your dream is to buy a Range Rover
Then you have to embrace excellence
Promotions are not gift hampers
To match up with your favourite Christmas Jumper
Every day you see your bills rise
At night you dream of a bumper pay rise
Cuddle up to excellence
As the days of buy one get one free are over
The big promotion sale to the unqualified is over
Mediocrity killed the firm in Andover
Ineptitude led to the collapse of the fly-over
Let excellence be your image and cover
And watch your Career goals come to fruition.

STOP THE STABBINGS

The uptick in the statistics of knife crime, killings and stabbings
is throbbing to all and sundry.
No one wants to be gone in their prime
before the audition of life even ever started.

I am on my way to work.
Police cars and forensic scientists form a barricade.
Another fatality
One more candle snuffed out.

There are days I dream of changing the world
In these times, I remember we have more pressing issues in our communities.
Knives. Gangs. Drugs
and youths sliding into the filth of crime.

I am screaming, STOP KNIVES ON LIVES.
So, you don't spend the core of your life in pokey.

LEAVE AND CLEAVE

All hail Mummy's boy
Still cannot let go of Daddy's toys
An advice from time to time
Leaves him with a mountain to climb
The instructions he can't do without
Are causing serious obstructions.

Leave and cleave
Just be brave
You proudly said I do
So why do you mistreat your boo
You married your wife
So why do you live in strife?

Mummy's darling girl
Grow up and be wise
She lived her life
Yes, that's right
Your marriage is not hers
Why carry your matter to her?

You fall and rise together
All your belongings you gathered
You make mistakes, learn, unlearn and relearn
No one needs a big mother hen
Leave and Cleave
So, we can truly enjoy this union.

TIME

Treasure your time
Like your most precious ornaments
Only give to those deserving
Causes so endearing
Value it like it means the world to you.

FIFTY AND BEAUTIFUL

She is fifty, nifty and beautiful
So beautiful the age does not say
Life begins when you want it to begin
How you react to life is entirely down to you

That's my feeling
Different folks
Different tales
Yours can have a happy ending

If you see things on the bright side
Trash every negative passenger on the ride
No matter the waves and tide
Always radiate happiness

as there is no room for loneliness
Fifty is beautiful, fifty is sexy.

ART

There are days I conjure a visit to the moon
with a parachute gliding through the sky
And my name etched in folklore
for greatness and good works.

There are days I travel in my mind
The border officer questions me, Can I see your passport?
I retort, I am on a journey
Between creative hemisphere.

The only visa required is time travel
My Art
Creativity
and everything in-between.

PUT A RING ON IT

Classy Couple
There is a rumble
He has been dating her for so long
Over five years that aches my lung
She warms his bed; that's so wrong
He uses her heart as ping-pong
Their love story could have been a love-song.

If you love her put a ring on it
The lies you tell her makes me sick
She is so lovable
To you she is gullible
She is adorable
You think it's all a fable
Don't waste away her glory.

In your folly
Put a ring on it
Or leave her to continue her journey
without you in it.

INTERTWINED

Your life and career are interwoven
like a newlywed couple in adoration
The anticlimax of a failed career
Is an ill-wind that can tear up a once happy soul.

There are days when my heart says
"Please walk!"
"Just quit this shit-hole of a job!"
My head whispers to my heart
"Your career is the **fulcrum** that holds the pieces of
your life together".

My head and heart are in a constant war
When I *reverie* about my bills
The Quest for subsistence
There can be only one champ.

My head is the calming force that gives connotation
To my life that would have been on the precipice
Of deprivation, want and hunger
If I left it to the rollercoaster emotions of my heart

I join my life and career in holy matrimony
Fused like a plug in a socket
Till death do us part.

RELIGIOSITY

We have been shackled with chains
In the gallows of religion
We spend our years in bondage and perpetual fear
of exalted men in the guise of cherubs.

There are days I burst into fits and hysterical laughter
at the filth and garbage
that has turned my father's house
into a theatre of comedy.

I hear some doctrines like half cooked beans
and I retract into my shell with alacrity
The slave masters long departed our shores
the only slavery left is religiosity perpetrated by those

who use the celestial realm as a gateway
to entangle us in the web of slavery.

THE FUTURE LEADERS OF TOMORROW

There are days I look into the future
and all I see is gross darkness, bleak and the *lust for power*
by the same leaders who have held us to ransom decade after decade.

The mantra of the youths being the future leaders of tomorrow has long been
forgotten.
No one says that any longer these days as we have become
a nation renowned for our recycling prowess.

We recycle nothing of note than politicians who have been on the scene
from the day I had an awareness of my existence.
Politicians and public office remind me of the day

I said I do to my *charming spouse*
Till death do us part.
These days we never hear of politicians' resignation.

Except by death.
The youths look on forlornly
The folly of the older cohorts' perpetuity in power leaves a bitter taste

in the mouth of unborn generations.
We are suffering and smiling
With no end to this madness in sight.

NIGERIA

A land flowing with milk, honey and oil
Our leaders have bled us dry, this is not funny
Roads filled with potholes
Streets abound with electric poles.

But no light
This is our plight
Few are taking flight
The majority take it in their stride.

With people renowned for being industrious
Yet poverty abounds in great proportions
A few live in luxury
The majority wallow in misery.

A tale of disparaging ends
Difficult indeed to comprehend
Lack in the midst of plenty
Hunger is the swansong of many.

Arise, the sleeping giant
Take your rightful place, remember you are not an ant
The world awaits the manifestation of your glory.

DREAMS THAT DIED

I dreamt of a better future
I was mocked that I built castles in the air.
I built dreams that came crashing down right before my very eyes.
The generator sound heralding the dark nights drowned
my ideas before it came alive.

My mind wanders off into dreamland
I am the Commander in Chief
I build roads, power, put food on the table
Back to reality.
This is awakening, we build survival before dreams.

Reality check two.
Dreams turned to ashes
Stillbirth.
Great dreams that died at incubation
the environment could not abhor.

Reality check 3
Capital flight in droves.
We build dreams not dust.
I weep
for all the dreams that died.

DANGERMAN

Big Bands
He is a dangerman
Not a loner
Let's say part of a groupie
That throng the loo
But don't wash their hands
They are a real danger
This is a serious clanger
Beware of the good morning
I know this sounds very funny
Behind the veil of the beautiful smiles
With the warm handshakes
Lies a ruthless pair
Of unwashed hands
This is the truth laid bare
Beware of the hands that you shake.

To: The Unwashed Hands after a visit to the Loo.

OPINIONS 2

Everyone has an opinion
Could be as many as the bulb in an onion
Your issues they want to pry
The truth is opinions are free
Everybody has one
When they come to you, please run
There is always a thought
An idea

On how we should live our lives
Some others want to help you fly your kite
They believe it's the new cool
Please don't be a fool
Or act like a tool
To be messed around
With ideas so profound

That might leave you confounded
To say the least dumbfounded.

NAMELESS

Let's call them nameless
The cold-blooded humans adorned with the toga of terrorists
that perpetuate barbarity with generous airtime
on satellite TV as a propeller.

Let's feed them with the fruit of abandonment
like a forsaken road after a severe thunderstorm
Throw them into the wilderness of obscurity
Rubbing them with the oil of disdain.

Let's treat them like an ill-wind that's up to no good
and adorn them with inscriptions
screaming
NAMELESS.

WOMAN

Truly human
Streams of Emotions
Rivers of Love
Flowing freely in the oceans of affection.

Woman
The grace to decipher
With pinpoint accuracy like a radio receiver
A selfless giver.

Take a deep breath
And celebrate
The wonderful woman
That adds colour to your world.

HAUNTED

Haunted by the ghosts of my past
My mistakes
Failures
And weaknesses

Devoured like a prey
In the oceans of fear
Sometimes I shed a tear
And run into my cocoon.

It's a new dawn
Another chance to be brave
Don't cave
To the negative voices.

Look into the mirror
Rewrite your story
Face your personal demons
Smile like a champion.

WALK WITH ELDERS

Walking with elders was ecstasy
Something to learn their words so tender
No matter how sophisticated
Cultured and swimming in the ocean of knowledge
A youth is
The realm of the elders remains sacred
Like a king decked in insignias on the throne.

I drink from the fountain of the aged
There are days I wear the regalia of wisdom
Off-loading the weight of my thoughts
On the altar of ignorance.
These days I walk with the elders
as there is always something to learn
Relearn and unlearn

A walk with the elders
Will leave you better.

WRITER'S BLOCK

You were my nightmare
Yes, you that unspeakable malaise
called writer's block.

CHAPTER 2

DEDICATED VERSES
& SPOKEN WORD CANTOS

UNCLE PIUS AND ETHIOPIA

Hide me under the wings of your shadow
Flames and fire
Shredded
Smoke and Ashes
Dreams kissed the dust with no goodbye.

To Ethiopia
That was not the utopia
Prayerfully renouncing a replica.

To Uncle Pius
Your legacy would be the impetus
that would engender social justice.

To the One Hundred fifty-seven lives lost
Take off
Landing amongst the heavenly.

You will never be forgotten.

*To: Professor Pius Adesanmi and the One Hundred and Fifty-Six humans that lost
their lives in the Ethiopia Airlines flight 302 on the 10th of March 2019.*

WHO AM I? (PART 1)

I am the best
Not like the rest
I am first
Amongst my peers
I am royalty
I don't need your loyalty
I am a king
Feel free to call me Lord of the rings
I face my fears
I don't do tears
I am talented
I am gifted
I am the light of the world
I choose my words
I am blessed
Christ has cleaned my mess
I don't dwell on the past
Enjoying my life like I do music on full blast
Adversity is a process in Life
With Christ I get to live my life right
I am a role model
You ain't seen nothing yet as I am still loading
The opinion of others doesn't define me
I soar on eagles' wings
I am good at what I do
I am beautiful
I appreciate my flaws
I don't in any way claim perfection
I am a child of the perfect one
I am who I say I am
I put my gifts to positive use
I plan to take a tour of the world like a ship on a cruise
I am free from the guilt of sin
Negative thoughts all in the recycle bin
I am free indeed
In words and in deed
I am who I say I am.

WHO AM I? (PART 2)

I am a victor
Not a victim
I have faced rejection
Negative news brought dejection
But I choose to hold on to God
Our love so strong it feels like a bond
I choose to live by faith
My God is never too late
The bad season is not my fate
He will work it out at his pace
I am a child of mercy
Life's problems so much, everything was messy
I wanted to give it all up
Please take it away, I hate this cup
My goal was to get to the top
Life's fiery darts thrown my way – that's what's up
No pain
No gain
It's a new season enjoying the new rain
Adversity made me strong, I'm no longer faint
I am who I say I am
Through life's raging storm I choose to be calm
The words I speak are a balm
Listen to me, O' Son of Man
I am the chosen one
Life's turned out to be so much fun
The night's no longer long
So close to the top-rung
I was first a fighter
My gift was to be a writer
So many battles I have won
So many times, I have been wrong
Countless times I have lost
The quest has always been to be first
I have made mistakes
Tried my best to be original
My life is mine to make
You are who you say you are: that is my take.

BLACK AND UNIQUE

I am black
I am unique
Unique with exceptional level of talents
Talents to contribute my quota to Accenture operations
Accenture operations does not discriminate on the basis of race
Work at your pace
As long as the target is ace
I look around me
Every day I see black men and women work tirelessly
Long hours
We take the work as if it's ours
At times all we eat is flour
Inclusion and Diversity is not a joke
Seclusion is not our culture
Exclusion not our values
Values for the world to see
I am black
I am unique.

*Written to celebrate Black History Month and Dedicated to the
Global Professional Services Company – Accenture.*

BANANA BREAD

I have some Banana Bread for you all
The email declaims
Bangalee
As generous as they come
True love is unstinting
Sharing the miniscule
To feed the horde
Entrenching an attitude
Of gratitude
And earning this platitude.

To: Aaron Lee, my friend from Red Clover.

NEWCASTLE – THE CITY
OF MY RISING STAR

I came to Newcastle
I had no plans to buy a castle
I came to work
If it doesn't work out,
I will take a walk
It's been a beautiful story
Look at me roaring
Newcastle, a city after my heart
Hear me out, I played my part
I have made great friends like David Roe
I only do friends, I don't need a foe
I love my life as a writer
Look at me, I am a fighter
Dreams come true
I will leave you with a clue
Headliner at the Stanza
No pain, no gain - this is my mantra
I love Newcastle
I am planning to buy a castle
Newcastle, the city of my rising star
Truth be told the future is bright
I will definitely go far
I am here to raise the bar
It's a marathon, not a dash
The writing community here is class
I doff my hat – you guys deserve top marks
Cheers to Newcastle, the City of my rising star.

To: Everyone who has shown me tremendous love in Newcastle.
Nigeria.

CRACKERS WITHOUT CHEESE

He eats crackers without cheese
Don't mention please
We all have our love-in
Don't try to tease me
Either way
With
Or without cheese
They all end up in our bowels
Then, the toilet
And the Land of no return.

Inspired by Linda Clow and the supporting cast
Olugbenga Obakin and David Wilson.

LETTER TO MY DEAR PARENTS

Wisdom unfettered
Like clothes spick and span
Words to make me better
Serenades me like a shelter
Fountain of knowledge
This is my pledge
To love you till the end of days
When the sun rays are no more
I will always cherish
The years you tutored
This has made me flourish
To my dear parents
Thanks for the love uncensored
For the sacrifices innumerable
For the memories
These are eternal
I will never forget
The times
The years
I wish you are here
With me
Forever.

To: My super dad and ever-loving mum – Gabriel & Temidayo Akinyemi

MAGICAL SAM

This is the assurance
When you need a soothing balm
Wipe your face with your palm
Relax
Take a deep breath
Be calm
And call on magical Sam
Gentle
Not from the clan of Gentiles
A beacon of peace
Tranquillity and Serenity.

To: Sam Sudan.

DAUGHTER

When your daughter asks you
why you treated her mother like a Queen?
tell her
you were teaching her never to lower her standards.

when your daughter asks you
why you were faithful to the end
tell her
you were teaching her never to settle for less.

To my daughter, Abigail.

ALEXANDRA

Strong beliefs
Defender of men
Passionate and priceless
Alexandra the brave
Always looking out for the good
Alexandra is my fave
Shining armour
A fighter and warrior
You talk about Alexander the Great
No please
Let's celebrate Alexandra the brave.

To: Alexandra Yeatman

STOP KNIVES ON LIVES

To my boys from the hood
Let's drop the knives
The killings
And the stabbings
Listen! I'm not blabbing
You have the chance to write your own story
Enough of the maiming
Counting scores
Putting out another's candle
All for the trivial
Look yourself in the mirror
You are destined for greatness
Not gangs
Drugs
Or the streets
Families weeping
Pain
Hurts
And sorrow abound
All around
Every day
Comes a sad tale
About knives
Cutting short lives
Let's put a stop to crime
In all its façade
Your future so bright
Like a soldier adorned on a parade
Let's do things right
With your strength
And might
Commit to be a positive light
A shining star
And all shades of amazing
Together we say no to crime
Knives
Stabbings
And slaughtering one another.

Inspired by Akinola Alabi – there is so much to achieve in the world than attacking one another with knives.

YOU ARE MY WOMAN

You are my woman
The one whom the hat fits
A million stars at the shining
So brightly in awe of how wondrously our love has grown
The angels sing in unison at your sight
Amused at the spectacular rise to be called one of them
In life and breathing
Through love and adoring.

I will always love you
In sunshine and sunsets
Your love permeates through my heart
I am captivated and mesmerized with your love
Two hearts entangled as one
The earth contracts and expands in salutation
To how our love has grown.

Dedicated to my Darling Wife, Olabisi

FORTY

Forty is the year of the dreamers
It's time to celebrate like a goal scored by Eden Hazard screamer
Forty could be described as an Art
It's time to play your part.

Forty could be described as a song
Composed by my favourite Artist
Can you hear the loud gong?
Relax, it's time to party.

Life begins at forty
Forty is the year of the achievers
Time to unleash your soaring eagle

Forty could be equated to an MC
The life of the show
Take a bow.

A toast to forty great years
This is my vow
Forty is a gift
Cheers to the next forty years.

SUNSHINE

You are my sunshine
The only reason I shine
You will always be mine
The only fruit on my vine.

No lies or deceitful lines
You are truly one of a kind.

To the one I chose forever

BLACK PICTURE

I am a Black Picture
I came on an adventure
To Accenture
To shape my future
Inclusion is part of their scriptures
Talent Pool, it's all a mixture
With a growing structure
It's all turned out to be a great venture
With lots of memories to treasure
Even when there is pressure
We do the work with pleasure
In winter or summer
No matter the weather
A place to work, not a conjecture
Truly a home for all the Black Pictures.

Written to commemorate Black History Month and Dedicated to the Global
Professional Services Company – Accenture.

CREATIVITY

Creativity is forever
Our imaginations are our greatest assets
Our minds, a brain box of ideas
Springing forth like the morning flower
Never despise the hen power
When our memories diminish
What remains with us forever is our imagination.

To: Equal Arts

A LOVE STORY MADE IN LIVERPOOL

A story made with love
Many decades ago this could not be foretold
Love is the language of the heart
Difficult to understand by the neutrals
Love is the rendition of the soul
Encapsulated by this coming together
Love is the symphony of our union
The silent harmonies
That echoes through the depth of our hearts
Love is the essence.

To: Biba & Nick – A love story made in Liverpool.

FRIENDS

Everyone needs great friends
Friends in the mould of Tom and Francis
So different from the famous Tom and Jerry
Always fighting over the bigger cherry
Who is Bash without the Rabs?
A little chick without its mother hen
Great friends are coverings
Protectors
And a shield
You are blessed if you have one
Daps and Obaks on a roller-coaster
In the good and bad
They stick together
We all need that special friend
That sticks closer than a brother
Not the ones that laugh with you
And scorn you in your absence
A slandering friend
Is as good as the enemy within.

Dedicated to Jolly Friends Thomas Braimah and Francis Okoli, Olugbenga Obakin and Oladapo Arofin and Abodunde Ojikutu and Rabiu Wasiu.

AUTHOR'S JOURNEY

There are puzzles and riddles authors fight off
like waging war against obscurity
Writing a book is no mean feat.

But, the majority of books
are cocooned in the shadows
with many building a home in the land of the forgotten.

There are days my books gaze at me in sobriety
Of a potential bestseller
whose lot is now the garage shed.

There is a thin line between success and failure;
any author who unravels this
has found their own garden of Eden.

To: Antonia Brindle of Get Brindled.

EVERY KING NEEDS A QUEEN

Every king needs a queen
Warm and receptive
We all need that special fellow
That can help us mellow
A charming glow
Like Evelyn's smile
As cool as the evening breeze
Ose's Mum
Osezua's Chum
Olabisi was my missing rib
Now found
I would say the missing link
Look at me kinging
From Hatfield
To Woolwich
To Manchester
Before we had a castle
In Newcastle
She was a true believer
In the days of the little
No tongue brittle
No words to tear down
All we got was love
A shoulder to lean on
When all we had was hope
Hope of a better tomorrow

Dedicated to Olabisi and Nubian Chic – Evelyn Aneni.
Osezua is an Esan name in South-South Nigeria which means
God chooses our home.
Ose is an Esan name in South-South Nigeria which means God.
Olabisi is a Unisex name in Yoruba culture of Southwestern Nigeria meaning Joy
is multiplied.

BABA SEVENTY

Baba Seventy
You ask me if I know your age
Please come out of your cage
It borders on the comical
At best a nuance
To harp on the trivial
As age is just a number
As the clock does tick tock
A summation of our years
Not our wisdom or intellect
A calculator of our time
Before the curtains are drawn
And we go to slumber
Age is just but a number.

BABA – in Yoruba, a language spoken by the Yoruba culture in the south western part of Nigeria, Baba is an honorific for father, wise man or, simply, elderly man.
To: Bandele Okunowo

ELIZABETH EDGAR

Elizabeth Edgar
A Queen amongst Queens
Of Royalty, Class and Grandeur
Grace and Elegance in abundance
Leadership skills top notch, not an amateur
With a smile that makes the heart melt
Simplicity a value.

Elizabeth Edgar
A leader of leaders
Compassionate and Loving
Strength of character, not a few
You came, you saw, you made your mark
The beautiful memories will forever linger
Au revoir Queen Eliz.

Dedicated to Elizabeth Edgar.

WE CAN BE THE SUNSHINE

We all need some sunshine
In a world of doom and gloom
Flourishing like flowers that bloom
We can spread love
Be gentle as a dove.

We all need some sunshine
Through life's unending curve
At times life can be tough
In times of despair
We can be the light like the rainbows appear.

We all need some sunshine
Through the cold, lonely days
We can be the sun rays
A beacon of hope
Truly this is dope.

We can be the sunshine
Through our little acts of service
It is expedient that we live a life of purpose
By giving the invaluable
Recreate memories memorable.

We can be the sunshine
By being kind to one another
In love we pamper
In deeds and words
Through those baby steps and little actions, we can change the world.

Dedicated to The Chronicle Sunshine Fund, First Performed at the Singing spreads Sunshine event for the Seaton Valley Schools at the Playhouse, Whitley Bay in June 2018.

FORWARD LADIES

Ladies are moving forward
this is not news
It doesn't matter your views
This is not limited to a few.

In the workplace;
ladies are moving forward
The era of a woman's place in the kitchen is now backward
Report abuse and violence; before you find yourself in the ward.

Ladies speak out and be bold
Always remember that you are more precious than Gold
The world belongs to us all
and you are a vital part of the fold.

Let your movement be forward
upwards and onwards.

*Dedicated to all Ladies Worldwide. Always remember that you
are more precious than Gold.*

DEAD DOGS DON'T BARK

Dead Dogs don't bark
The bark of a Dog reverberates
Not muffled
The plan is to leave you ruffled
Beware of Dogs
The gate signs read
Fear and trembling, my body sank
That is a warning
Of the prowess of a living dog
While we are here
And at it
Let the world hear your bark
Be a bright spark
Make a difference
Let your name resonate
Take a walk of glory
Stand up tall
Don't be in the shadows
Leaving the world unknown
The same way you came
Drinking from the streams of mediocrity
Don't be a tourist
When you could have been the pilot
Living on purpose
Getting your hands on the plough
Just like the moonlight tales of old
Be the hero
The last man standing
The warrior who endured till the very end
Remember
A living dog is better than a dead lion
Dead Dogs Don't Bark
They are a mere carcass
All their glory laid to waste
Dead Dogs Don't Bark
And they don't bite.

YAYA TOURÉ

He set the Premier League alight
Not willing to surrender without a fight
Some lazy defenders took flight
Managers sorry at their plight.

Yaya, an epitome of strength
Always drenched in sweat
Free kicks always swerving into the net
Everyone's favourite to win a bet.

Africa's true son
Allow me to blow his horn
His light shone like a star
Shone brightly from near and afar.

A supporter of other talents, never nonchalant
A warrior in his own right, so gallant
A true African hero
A story of a top man who came from ground zero.

Dedicated to Yaya Touré; a true African Legend.

KARL GOT LUCKY

Karl is getting lucky
Lucky to have an angel in a world I call murky
Every man needs a princess
To take away all the stress.

Karl is getting lucky
Lucky to have a jewel, he is so happy
It's a new dawn so bright like Sunday morning
The future looks awesome with so much money.

Karl is getting lucky
This is a warning to the single ladies lurking
Just say the golden words if you are burning
Let me reiterate this is not funny.

Karl is getting lucky
Exiting the singles club, he has done a running
Being single has never been a calling
So much in love he is practically falling.

Karl is getting lucky
Put on your dancing shoes, it's time to get funky
Marriage could be so much fun
Two is indeed better than one.

Karl is getting lucky
Everyone is fully dressed, looks like we are balling
We all wish you marital bliss
Love so sweet forever cling.

To: Lucky & Karl.

THE HEAD

You are the head, yes, we know
Why all the fuss that **heads will roll?**
You are the head, yes, we know
Why always blow **hot and cold?**

You are the head, yes, we know
Why always say it as if we **need to know?**
You are the head, yes, we know
Why so much beating as if we **have same strength?**

You are the head, yes, we know
Why so much abuse to **bring me down?**
You are the head, yes, we know
Why not treat me **as a partner?**

You are the head, yes, we know
Why not listen before **you self-destruct?**
You are the head, yes, we know
Take a trophy; hope this **massages your ego.**

Dedicated to the man that never listens.

PREGNANT

You are pregnant
Pregnant with dreams that can change the world
You are pregnant
Pregnant with ideas money cannot buy.

You are pregnant
Pregnant with goals that could turn around your fortunes
You are pregnant
Pregnant with possibilities as impossibility is not an option.

Get your vision into motion
Greatness is your portion
Don't be part of the numbers
That spent their years in slumber.

Don't let the distractions of the world encumber
Your hands on the plough like a mathematician solving a formula
Go forth into the delivery room
It's your time to bloom.

As the hidden treasure is set to be delivered.

LADY TESS

Lady Tess
A Queen so blessed
It's your birthday, a time to flex
Let's forget the stress.

Lady Tess
Daddy's Queen, no one else
A virtuous woman her children called her blessed
Life's like a book, not a game of chess.

Lady Tess
We don't do no mess
Honour her armour like a Gold crest
Amongst her peers she is first.

To: Tessy Olagunju, the sugar in the tea of Hakeem Olagunju.

PERFECT GENT

The idiosyncrasies of some alpha males should only be left unsaid
All of my life
I have had dreams of being a perfect gent
I was raised by a king

A man of honour.
Brick upon brick
I am building the layers and foundations
Called rock solid.

I look at the dynasty.
Game on
Only perfect gents abide in this home
Not yet *eureka*.

I am **work in progress**
In my quest to be a **perfect gent**.

To: Adam Gent – The Perfect Gent.

BADDOSNEH

The white man eats our Jollof
His face in sheer delight
Isi ewu was wolfed in a hurry
The barriers have been broken
The pangs of hunger know no colours.

The white man speaks our language
My face lights up with a glow
The barriers of superiority
Forever shattered
No more gusts of inferiority.

Unless to those who have been
Entangled in perpetual slavery.

*To: Stewart Evans – He is one of us, nicknamed Baddosneh due to his love
for the Nigerian Culture, Baddosneh is the nickname of Olamide, a popular
indigenous rap artist in Nigeria.
Isi ewu is a traditional Igbo dish that is made with a goat's head.*

SARAH GARTON

An epitome of compassion
Humility in leadership not an aberration
Competitive for excellence
The results can tell.

Like Sarah in the Bible times
Her husband's delight
The young ladies cannot go wrong
A friend of all, we the people throng.

A Goal Getter
As the years pass by, she gets better
A victor over all of life's adversity
An overcomer that we can proclaim certainly.

She lights up the room with a charming glow
An impactful life the world needs to know
A role model is here
Let the young ones hear.

Sarah Garton
She is always ready to pass the baton.

Dedicated to Sarah Garton – An Inspirational Leader.

BROWNIE

The Gentleman is asking: can I be your crown?
Dark cookie like my favourite brownie
Beauty that tells a million stories
The one who deserves you will truly flourish
I am ready to spend all my savings at the florist.

Intelligence speaks
I see you getting to the peak
Beauty with Brains that's fleek
Truth be told she is meek
The future's so Bright, no way, it can't be Bleak

The golden girl of her generation
You truly deserve the acceleration
This is my proclamation
The pride of her nation
This is my legislation.

To the Intelligent One: Anthonia Brown.

DISTANCE

Your main issue was distance
When all you had to do was take a stance
You made loving you a farce
My Queen was away and took a stand.

Through this she strengthened our bond
Sweet memories forever fond
I will never forget she is one of a kind
A treasure so hard to find.

Love they say is blind
With you I won't mind
Distance is not a curse
Let's not make so much fuss.

The right woman who takes a stance
Always shines brightly like a star.

To my darling wife, a virtuous woman who deserves a crown.

IT WAS LOVE

Through the years
The melody of my heart
The vows exchanged
For better
for worse
Till death do us part
It wasn't just a mere rhetoric
I do

Was the recital
Far from the ritual
The habitual
Of every Ade, Jade, and Demi
Love was the driver
Flowing through like a river
Love was the encyclopaedia of my soul
Love was the Anthem.

To: Oluwaseun and Isaac A.

TOLUTOLUDO

Tolu is getting blessings
My life's storm has taught me some lessons
To never give up without a fight
Even when circumstances do not look right.

Tolu is getting favoured
My life so sweet like a fragrance to savour
Not so long ago I could be likened to a prey the lions wanted to devour
I have waved my problems bye, it's Au revoir.

Tolu is getting blessings
Upward, onwards, it's time to get flexing
In strange places I have enjoyed mercy
I have only just started, I feel thirsty.

Tolu is getting famous
Smile so beautiful so contagious
I am on the rise
Onwards and upwards.

To higher heights.

Through this poem I celebrate my journey, story and achievements.

SURULERE

Patience is a virtue
So rare
A trait
Found amongst the greats
A gift
Displayed by the wise
The patient person
Always has a reward.

A prize
For going over and above
As many through impatience
Have missed out on golden opportunities
Be patient
Wait for it
And you will earn a reward someday.

Surulere – means patience has a reward.

YOUNG AND LOST

I was once young and lost
My life so filled with my lust
I tried to put myself first
Loved the glam life that was my thirst.

Boys around that was my crush
Ego so big no one can brush
My youth spent in darkness
Eyes opened my talent I now harness.

Dreams so big
Like fruits on a fig
Left the binge
Too much drink now makes me cringe.

Learn from me
Eyes opened now I can see
Living my dreams
Lots of energy busting at the seams.

My talent put to use
Young and lost now a ruse.

To: Hena Bryan – Super proud of you.

MENTAL HEALTH

Health is wealth
Don't be afraid to offer help
We all go through some form of stress
It's important to take a rest.

Health is a gift
Don't be afraid to be a bridge
There are days when we feel down
Speak out as soon as you can.

Life's situation like the turbulent wind
Nine to five daily on the grind
Daily survival is what we find
Our mental health should be top of the pile.

THE SPECIAL ONES

This is for the special ones
The ones who were happy to do some rounds
In seasons when I got started
Like a lone voice
In the wilderness
These were the ones that gave us cover
At the speed of light like a Range-Rover
I soared like an eagle
The aim was to reach the pinnacle
The race is not for the fickle
O' what sheer delight
When you have brothers in arms
Sisters once unknown
Strategists uncensored
All to build the brand
Even if I have a million grand
I can't repay you for the chants
For lending your voices
To help me grow
Hoping someday I will blow
I hope you will someday read these words
Written from my heart
Hope this lightens your faces
And please know you are truly special
To me.

To everyone that has supported me and my brand, to everyone who has sown words of affirmation and truly believed in my talent, my unique voice and the fire that burns in my belly.

ACCIDENTAL VEGETARIAN

You claim you are a vegetarian
But at night you go home to a plate of Akpu and Okro soup
You claim you only do veggies
But on the odd days you are tempted by the meatballs and pepperoni pizza
You claim you are a vegetarian
But it's only a show-off
On the day you have no food
And can't be bothered to cook
You claim you are a vegetarian
But sometimes you devour a plate of fried rice with chicken
You claim you are a vegetarian
In truth we know it's a façade
To blow up your ego
We won't forget the chronicles of Raw Nirvana and the fish in Bali
and the sordid tales of premenopausal
the false life of pretence and deception like shattered eggs
Unravelled in a canter
And we all know you are not a vegetarian
But an accidental vegetarian.

To: The Accidental vegetarian.
Akpu is a Nigerian food, a wet paste made from cassava, and Okra (Okro) Soup
is a farm fresh soup recipe prepared with green vegetables.

FOZIAH

Beautiful like a work of art
So radiant like my favourite painting
Smile so beautiful the angels' delight
Compassionate, loving and doting.

Mancunian Queen
No airs
Gentle as a dove
Wisdom that surpasses her years.

Foziah
So classy
Sassy
And Ballsy.

To: Foziah – Bright spark, keep on shining.

IRETIOLUWA IS THIRTY

Iretioluwa is thirty
On the way to greatness she looks thirsty
A virtuous woman, Olusegun's Bestie
A life of honour not in any way messy.

Growing up she was different
Her report card was a point of reference
Her middle name was excellence
So, loving with a heart of benevolence.

In school she was always top
Eyes on the goal, nothing could stop
Intelligent Queen, this is not floss
Steadily on her way to being boss.

A goal getter with pinpoint accuracy like Frank Lampard's lob
A Chelsea fan, the best London Club
She's shining so bright like your fluorescent light bulb
Bearing fruits like growing stems shrub.

Rejoice, it's thirty great years
The future looks bright, no more fears
Joy unending, no more tears
Cheers to many more amazing years.

To my darling and only sister "Iretioluwa" at Thirty.

PEER PRESSURE

Let's snub peer pressure
Live life to your own pleasure
Like clothes sewn to measure.

Don't be led astray
And be a prey
Have your say.

Follow your heart
Your intuition
Feel free to make your own decisions.

Let these words guide you
It's your life and your call
Write your own song and blow your gong.

Don't be swayed by indecisions
And peer pressure.

EKITI STATE

I am from the fountain of knowledge
I see it as a privilege
I am an offspring of the brilliance
That pervades our landscapes.

I am from the land of the intellectuals
Renowned for our sagacity
Don't mind my audacity.

I am a brain box of ideas
From the fountain of knowledge.

Ekiti State: Is a state in the South-Western part of Nigeria popularly called Fountain of Knowledge and renowned for the Academic brilliance of her people. I am from Ekiti and Proud. From Alfred to Gabriel to Tolulope – three Generations of Akinyemi and the name is waxing strong.

BIO

Tolu' Akinyemi is an exceptional talent, out-of-the box creative thinker; a change management agent and a leader par excellence. Tolu' is a business analyst and financial crime consultant as well as a Certified Anti-Money Laundering Specialist (CAMS) with extensive experience working with leading Investment Banks and Consultancy Firms. Tolu' is also a personal development and career coach and a prolific writer with more than 10 years' writing experience. He is a mentor to hundreds of young people. He worked as an Associate Mentor in St Mary's School, Cheshunt and as an Inclusion Mentor in Barnwell School, Stevenage in the United Kingdom, helping students raise their aspirations, standards of performance and helping them cope with transitions from one educational stage to another.

A man whom many refer to as "Mr Vision", he is a trained Economist from Ekiti State University formerly known as University of Ado-Ekiti (UNAD). He sat his Masters' Degree in Accounting and Financial Management at the University of Hertfordshire, Hatfield, United Kingdom. Tolu' was a student ambassador at the University of Hertfordshire, Hatfield representing the University in major forums and engaging with young people during various assignments.

Tolu' Akinyemi is a home-grown talent; an alumnus of the Daystar Leadership Academy (DLA), he is passionate about people and wealth creation. He believes so much that life is about impacting on others. In his words, "To have a Secure Future, we must be willing to pay the Price in order to earn the Prize".

Tolu' has headlined and featured in various Open Slam, Poetry Slam, Spoken Word and Open Mic events in the United Kingdom. He also inspires large audiences through spoken word performances, he has appeared as a keynote speaker in major forums and events in the United Kingdom and facilitates creative writing masterclasses to all types of audiences.

Tolu' Akinyemi was born in Ado-Ekiti, Nigeria and currently lives in the United Kingdom. Tolu' is an ardent supporter of Chelsea Football Club, London.

You can connect with Tolu' on his various Social Media Accounts:

Instagram: @ToluToludo
Facebook: facebook.com/toluaakinyemi
Twitter: @ToluAkinyemi

AUTHOR'S NOTE

Thank you for the time you have taken to read this book. I do hope you enjoyed the Poems in it and you are ready to find your Unique Bark and Spark.

If you loved the book and have a minute to spare, I would really appreciate a brief review on the page or site where you bought the book. Your help in spreading the word is greatly appreciated. Reviews from readers like you make an enormous difference to helping new readers decide to get the book.

Thank you!
Tolu' A. Akinyemi

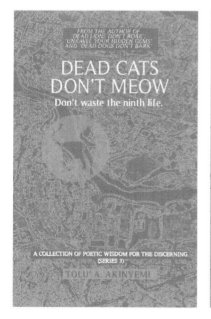

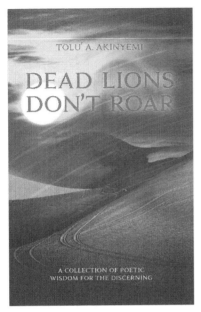

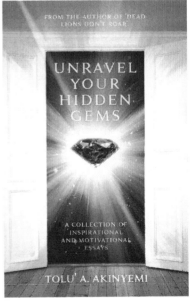

Printed in Great Britain
by Amazon